FOUL PAPERS

PETER PEGNALL

Belfast
LAPWING

First Published by Lapwing Publications
c/o 1, Ballysillan Drive
Belfast BT14 8HQ

Copyright © Peter Pegnall 2005
Copyright Cover Image © Jo Pegnall 2005

The author has asserted her/his right under Section 77
of the Copyright, Design and Patents Act 1988
to be identified as the author of this work.

British Library Cataloguing in Publication Data.
A catalogue record for this book is available from
the British Library.

Set in Aldine 721 BT
by
Winepress Services

ISBN 1-905425-31-7

CONTENTS

FOUL PAPERS

PETER PEGNALL

To

Edna Pegnall

Foul papers

My nana kept chickens, I loved to filch the eggs,
giggled when they fussed and pecked in the dirt.

Somehow they seemed like her, feathered in busy-ness -
but who was I to know what happened beneath her dress?

In the sun lounge there were cacti
and once, one flowered.

Thank god for that.

A Piece of Peace

I've driven miles and miles in this country,
no little way in Ireland, France, Portugal
even swooped through the Tuscan moon-hills,
sashayed across Westchester County
clambered Macbeth's frozen wastes, sat locked
in Essex, squeezed into the Great West Road
You think I'll go on and on?
          Rest assured, rest easy,
rest and rest, as I drive, radio on,
king-cat shades perched before my odd eyes
and come to rest at Cliviger, where the trees
remember England before the Conqueror
where the roe deer gambol, where harebells sway,
where sparrowhawks share the sky with kestrels,
peregrine falcons and the bold wheatear.

You'd love it, Ken, you'd growl with pleasure,
a bit of a rare creature yourself, a bit
of an AngloSaxon, a bit of a Celt,
a bit of a wild man of the woods
but no club in your hand, no pelt round your loins,
only the justified anger of one·
to whom greater harm has come than he's caused
would ever cause in a thousand years
of blood-boltered history. We need soldiers like you,
we are bereft, temporarily, we lack
the strong shoulder, the belly laugh,
the sessile oak of old England. But we'll wait.
Take your time. Rest easy. The wind is in the heather,
the willow bends for joy of springtime.

And then they wank us off

For Julius Howard Nussbaum

'this is my friend Julius, he's a Jew'.
My grandmother nearly fell off the settee
or would she have called it the sofa?
Anyway, we were a motley crew,

You Francis and I. With Smellis on the fringe,
Tim Partner the best team captain and Mutton
no doubt a millionaire now. Do you recall
him looking in the mirror and hurting?

That's in the past. Why do you hurry so much?
Why do you disrespect your present tense?
You've done far less harm than others think;
calm down. Love the one you're with. See sense.

Your plasma screen's on the blink,
you can't even breathe for cough.

Best Mate is dead

His first Cheltenham race, I won fifty quid,
Went to the Hole in the Wall and downed some sherbies.

Felt all right. Had heard about him on radio.
I don't make a habit of betting, but now and then
I'll splash out. The best time by far
Was on the Santander ferry when I put my last coin
In the fruit machine and the coins flowed out
Like a golden cataract. 200 of them.

Now that's what I'd call lucky, unlike
That poor, beautiful beast. Think of his shiny, handsome head.

No Dog Dave

Has no trousers, walks the streets in skinny legs,
has drunk the whole bottle: now it's dregs.

Has a son who sails the high Hokusai waters.
As far as I know has no daughters.

Likes a bet. Hasn't won yet, but once
came second at Plumpton. Thinks he's a dunce,

but I imagine he's adequately clever.
I never saw his dog. Never ever.

Poetry Workshop

Jake can't write, *broken me finger* he says
Molly hangs her head, folds her arms, listens.
Muzaffar isn't allowed Christmas,
scratches out secret letters to Santa.

Please make my dad come home. There are rats
in the coalhouse and one of them's my uncle.
Molly hoards wordplay, keeps it safe,
her other place to be. Jake sneaks a look

at Molly's poem. It's crisp as icing sugar,
frivolous as tinsel; he saves his love,
zooms into the playground, swoops on Muzaffar,
an eagle glutted on words, a velvet glove.

To an Unborn Child
For Adrian and Eliza Nash

You're the Mekon in a cradle of blood,
a goblin in a rocking chair,
an astronaut in light years of space,
a cherub with curly hair.

You're everything that makes us good:
Maid Marian, Robin Hood.

Enough

Downstairs there's a party going on,
whoops of competitive merriment,
hugger-mugger conversations. Someone
ragtimes the old upright, a young poet
rolls a skinny fag, parts her sweet lips,
translates boredom into cabaret,
nothing to say her trademark enticement.

Outside, sequins blink through dark purple,
love finds a doorway, a cold, comfortable place,
quick-thrilled by midnight's secret noises.

But here there is only the pen across the page,
a dripping tap. Here is where the forbidden
'I' crafts a place to stand, despite the spell
of side by side. It will be like this, I guess,
when sex falls away, the strong hand of friendship
loses grip. Sufficient to begin with breath,
that unchosen first, final rhythm,
sufficient to rise and fall without comment,
without complaint. To wave as you go.

The Navigator

I see you, there, with a rose in your teeth
One more thin gypsy thief
                    Leonard Cohen, Famous Blue Raincoat

It was a poppy, in fact, as you skedaddled
Towards the bar at The White Lion.
Charmer supreme, patent shoes, manicured moustache,
You'd set your table for a new Zion,
Flanked by cheap offers in the Co-op.
You remember and therefore you survive:
Even that last comb of the hair marks respect.

You made my mum feel seventeen again,
After years of hunger and neglect.
A man like you rises above the shop,
Flies into the heart, like a snazzy jive.

When the plane nose-dived, it was Norman who paddled,
When the enemy attacked, Norman bore the lash,
Or he flashed down the Matterhorn like James Bond,
A lethal weapon, although a little round.

A. and E.

Sooner or later we all make it here;
curling posters, last summer's magazines,
safe wooden infant playspace. We're centre stage
and supporting cast from coffee machine

to tubular chair, compete in grimace.
Just round the corner there's someone worse off
face withered into pain beyond pretence.
Cue the crazy-angled arm, volcanic cough,

why does that man nearly remind me of me?
Where has that woman hidden her other leg?
An hour passes, a few more graveyard jokes,
the ragtag gang outside, dying for a smoke.

The woman with purpled eyes and crooked jaw
shrieks: 'I'm off home! You can't do nothing for me!'
Bloody right. She's addicted to his fists,
wheels herself away to get very pissed.

A Jar of Pickles
For Gaia Holmes

I give you what's left of my right lung:
let it breathe at last, as red chillies
glide through the sponge like tropical fish,
as black peppers bob in vinegar,
muscovado granules sweeten the rot.

Place the jar proud on your piano,
serenade a lost part of me,
plunk away with liquid fingers,
pierce the long night with stranger song.

Recipes for surprise, your poems
roll over my tongue like burgundy,
preserve the flesh we wear for a while,
seal sighs and hunger on a clean white sheet.

'I'm Dying Soon': Freya Rogers, aged 4

Not until you've picnicked in the forest
where the light breaks across the green shadows,
where a dog paddles in clear water
and bluebells nod a last, hazy goodbye.

And not until you've held your own daughter's hand
as you stroll the shoreline of the ceaseless sea,
and you wonder. Not until you've loved and left,
sung and suffered, faced the steep climb of morning
twenty five thousand times. Not yet, my dear one.

Dried out

Ten days without a drink; hard to tell moment
from moment, suck any kind of sweetness,
roll words around the tongue. We must rejoice
beyond reason, intoxicate on air,
imagine ice crackle in amber whisky,
breathe tipsy love in warm delighted ears.

Right now I'd be afloat in my sixth glass,
on the sharp edge of another wisecrack,
glad to find friendship where it finds me,
another round, then that spiral. I'll be back,
as the bright days of blossom outside pass,
leaves waft in currents of winter glee.

Jingle Jangle

If you like a lot of chocolate
on your biscuit, join our club
It's 2.30 and the silly tune
bounces back and forth in your brain.
Bank managers, chiefs of police,
accusing lovers queue up on the stairs.
Your dead dad's face peeks through the curtain:
you've let me down badly this time.
Then the disappearing talent act:
you'll never write another line.
It's all hospital beds and daytime TV
now on in, years and years to bore down,
sauced with haemorrhoids, gritted with guilt.
If you like a lot of chocolate
stalks you downstairs, cats ambush your legs,
clogged dishes Tracey Emin the sink
and whose dread voice lurks on the answer phone?
Back in bed you find your face
in all the small-minded scoundrels in Dickens
and you sweat the slow-motion minutes
until a dream reminds you you're on stage next
and can't remember a single line.
Does Hamlet fancy a lot of chocolate
on his biscuit? Why don't the others guess
you're a fraud? Where are your trousers?
And why does *sorry seem to be the hardest word?*

Easter Eucharist in a Norfolk Village

We must need healing. Why else stand side
by side in an ancient stone cross?
mumble confession, cry to be at one
at last? Encased in freshly-baked hair-styles,
singing together never so solitary.

Each knows his place in this castaway refuge:
whose garland fringes the pulpit, whose voice
garbles Isaiah, who passes the plate,
gathers the hymn books, serves the Nescafe.
Hope lurks somewhere. Is it in the last anthem,
one more torn petal in the daisy chain of days?

I'd like to think that a deep spring of love
swells through these woolly berets, these weary hearts,
that an awful mystery binds us, even
as we turn away. Redemption's too large
to last for more than a moment.

like a love bite

1.

like a love bite
        I've got you under my skin
Geraldo and the boys blow hot and sweet,
it's ladies' night at The Midland Hotel:
spinning circles of chiffon, staccato feet,
cottage loaf hairdos, a suffocating whiff
of *Evening in Paris*, of submarine sin.

Faces wink in the glitter ball. Pauline
lights a Consulate, sips a gin and lime,
wishes herself on someone else's arm
as her squat husband counts his change. Wishes
Morecambe under the waves, wishes a storm
in their suburban nest, a shatter of dishes,
eruption of u-bends. Feels lost and mean.

Eric unbuttons his dj, struts like a duck
towards the last wallflower on the left,
his head shines, his shoes shine, his teeth shine plastic.
She follows him into the foxtrot, glad
and resigned. He swerves like a skater, deft,
a featherweight at fifteen stone. She's sick
with desire, with delight, with forty years unfucked.

2.

Tables are still laid. White damask, red napkins,
heavy silverware. The staircase swirls around
like a flamenco: a fat benefactor
gazes down on his palace of fun. No sound,

only the thin wind through the grimy glass,
only the sigh of the shallows in the bay,
only Roderick's feet trailing down the prom.
He'd never asked her. Not known what to say.

And she's long dead and the Midland Hotel's
squatted by rats and smack heads. The gay mural
laughs without mirth at the cobwebs and dust
and this white ocean liner's laced with rust.

Then said I:
'Ah, Lord God! Behold I cannot speak: for I am a child'
(Jeremiah 1.6)

In memory of Jeffrey Nuttall and for his family

Ride your exercise bike into eternity,
Jeff. Roar your lion-laughter, raise your trilby,
conquer a mountain side of bangers and mash.
empty a tarn of Timothy Tailors, splash
dollops of mustard on your maroon cravat,
dance down the road past the cemetery. You're not fat,
you're generously upholstered. Speak to us now,
blow your cornet at its Sunday best, sow
our toxic fields with wild strawberries, zinnia, beans.
madcaps of mischief. Now is the poet's time,
now, whilst critics inscribe what we mean to mean,
package is substance, nature a theme park,
savage indignation almost a crime:
speak to us *as a child cries out in the dark.*

A Late Love Song to Ms. Rossetti

Sick at heart, Christina opened her lips,
carolled harsh beauty. Her stiffened suitors
didn't match up; sisterhood held her down,
a strangle of love, of duty, second place.
Goblin Market was not the order of the day.

All the more succulent, her giddy journey,
her lavish, other world seduction.

What would you say, Christina, if I dropped by?
would we take tea in porcelain cups?
Chew neat triangles of toast and honey?

I shall learn Italian, wear wing collars,
intone nightly *Hymns Ancient and Modern*,
suppress my animal. You're worth the wait,
even as grapes wrinkle, cherries rot.

Between Heaven and Charing Cross
With an anachronistic nod to Francis Thompson on the streets of London.

December in Trafalgar Square. Pavements slopped
with leaves, leaflets, tomato skins. Headlong
the crowd pours onwards, sliced by taxis,
splattered by buses, side by side unspeaking.

His overcoat ventilated. His shoes
flap and wink. You might not choose to stroke his hair.
He dips into The National Gallery,
warms himself at Van Gogh's 'Sunflowers', can't help
but blurt God and Isleworth when two students
place their lazy loveliness between the bench
and his master's furrowed faces. His voice
doesn't match his trousers. They squeal and scamper,
scream aloud his madness and his stench.

No need for the glazed attendant. Exit,
to a fanfare of small farts, like a scooter,
the soggy sound of how far he'd fallen.

At first it seemed the music was memory,
lament as heartstrung as combed hair,
ripples of touch, silver racing raindrops;
how could he know the music was hers,
curled round the light behind the curtains,
the curtains a riot of threadbare roses?
How could he guess she was fleshy as sin,
that she called to him, through a door that closed
on the sluice of the past?
                              Another shot,
then sleep wherever he slumped. Not tonight,
not if she could help it. She'd opened herself
to sticky plantations, fumble and grope
of stubby fingers, abuses and bruises,
to ingenuities of lust, to losers
and lawyers. This scarecrow poet, gentle man,
restored, for a while, her music. So she sang.

Sent his poems to The London Magazine,
left him with something more than modest fame,
occasional good health: left him almost clean,
left him longing for more, carved out in half-rhyme.

Viva El Bigote!

In loving memory of Ken Smith

That moustache could fly the Atlantic,
sweep clean the Bakerloo Line, congeal lunch,
breast the waves like a cormorant. Romantic,
buccaneering, cantankerous. Packs a punch
as you flail mist on mist, as you grip
Judi, island queen of your return
ticket. I think I've glimpsed how life can strip
a man, maroon him. But found no way to learn
what's left, when words spin and dip, like a rogue
Zapata over the Irish sea, over
Buncrana, where your deadlocked father's vague
birthleap lay dumb. Ken Smith, real Irish Rover,
follow your paintbrush into another spring:
bushy grey butterfly, flag of freedom, rebel king!

What it's like now

The shed's falling down. Inside, two bikes,
a green plastic patio set, piles and piles
of paper. Poems, letters, essays - crumpled,
fading, urgent copy kept in the dark.

In the windows, clouds swim like fat white cherubs,
farm houses crouch in hazy geometry,
my face looks back at me, silent and creased
as the buried papers. Something's different.

Something about walking away as if
I wanted to. As if it's necessary.
Something about how sitting here now
isn't what it was last week. One by one,
I'll count up the minutes on my own. Regret
not mending the shed, regret not putting my hand
to the past. Rehearse perfect meals out here,
under the August sun, October stars,
meals we didn't eat. Raise a glass to the reflection.

I wasn't too happy about the abortion

Our boy's out on the wall. His floppy hat's
flown away, his maraschino eye's gone,
his raisin nose a brown hole. But his grin,
his thin, lemon peel grin, that's still there.
And his stubby arms reach out, his buttons
mark his fat belly, he dances to wind song,
conducts skittish snowflakes, stands firm against
the night. We know our warm love would kill him.

And so, ten years ago, melted away,
a signature on a form, a better life
without this life? Out in the cold, a white shape.

whereas in this life, nothing is sure and certain

you kept your eyes on the meat, chopped
expertly. you'd only once or twice rest
your hazel beauties on my odd pair.
i asked if you were a poet. you demurred
and who was the fool then? behind me,
an old man in a white skirt, silent.

is that what you get for living so long?

you said we had to struggle
with our souls, that our souls worked against us.
what on earth did you mean?
'this vegetable,'
you said,' this long, green dildo, ridged,
carbuncled, glorious green. this is bitter,
must be cooked separately. but so must
all these magical fruits, the purple bells,
the green torpedoes, the red buttocks.'

for, as in life, nothing is sure and certain,
otherness is all there is. if that's
ancient sufic wisdom, I'll drink to it,
pour a glass for you, learn to speak your name.

The land's so flat …
                you can see your dog leaving you for three days

At first he busied himself with needless chores.
unpacked those books in the attic, read letters,
the letters hurt. He made many cups of tea,
barked at the meek man from the gas company,
collapsed into the uneasy chair,
relic of a penal tramp around IKEA.
Demon of the remote control, he fast-flicked
celebrity chefs into oblivion,
scanned The Guardian's pious bleat, took umbrage,
failed yet again to relish Karamazov.

Once, he went to the window, saw the shape
framed in silver light. Whether it went on,
stood still, returned, he preferred not to think.
Preferred also not to think why? Plunged into
ghost-written rhetoric, hung-up harangues,
puling laments. Then, at last, *thwunk* goes the cork
and deep, purple goblets of wine. The shape
smaller, now, skeletal. So the days drained through,
imperceptibly, fatally different,
the bed Saharan, birdsong dark laughter.

Ray's a Laugh

With a face like an ordinance survey map,
eyes like murky pools
and clothes in a dozen shades of brown

Ray is not a man you'd take to the dance.

But were you to wish to question
the nature of the atom, or why rainbows
arc our unhappy lives

he might participate for a polite minute.
Otherwise he'll sit above his half pint
and stare.

As if you weren't there.

Dark

I'm reading Dostoyevsky in my shorts;
late September, fat apples thump on the grass,
I dunk my Arrowroot in Assam,
glimpse a pair of wood- pigeons peck and fondle.
This is the way to crack philosophy,
stretch faith to its last fibre, invite the storm:
comfortable's the best way to be uneasy.

Three days ago there were sirens in my head,
ferrets in my gut, I slid off the ground
where I stood. I'm surprised they let me loose,
forgave my trespasses. Get this straight:
these terrified voices make no sound,
do not disturb. You're on your own. What's the use?

On the tiles

Last night Haruki Murakami hit town;
we cruised Old Compton Street, a couple of swells,
downed a few large ones, spoke of butterflies,
suicide, the honeycomb heart of the crunchie bar.

He vanished, my elfin twin
and yet again I fingered solitude
loved the Soho sky so bright with unanswered cries.

In Portugal there's a little town called Purgatorio

Today, at last, I shall wash. Autumn clean the house,
scrape my beard away, swirl the iron filings down the plughole,
expel the cats for a fresh hour or two. Then I shall face the screen,
be prepared to smudge a little light on what I don't like:

sexual tightropes; the young boy I was, shoved back on a bed,
Roy's sausage fingers at work on my half-blind penis,
fear and shame and pleasure blanked out. He was bald and big,
leered with gusto at the seafood stink of women.

So when I lay with my teenage sweet heart and hung limp,
I sensed there was something wrong with me, something that hated,
something bad enough to blight years and years to come.
Something that almost went in my wife's arms, and I thank her,
although I'd guess the 'almost' divided us,
almost as much as her love for women.

For too long now I've loved what I've lost. Who I've lost.
Lost as in no longer together as one
at least as long as for the nights.
This is as clear as the scruffy beard on my face,
my taste for too much wine, for being adored,
somewhat. And it's not the stuff of a poem,
but may be the stuff of good intentions never quite fulfilled,
as boring as that. Back to the Electrolux, the Gillette.

Not Having Lunch at Shibden Mill

The starter was antipasto of air,
a Tuscan treasure. The main course wasn't there.

For dessert, a desert of waiting
and it was then we began contemplating

rebellion. How not very English
to lunch on anger, a dyspeptic dish.

Not for the Last time

For Paula

I love autumn in Hyde Park: the taxi
skids past the Serpentine -
I was a serpent myself, next to you,
pointed at the glister of Albert's memorial:

despair and money
in one sun kissed, vulgar gesture.
How does grief say itself?

We saw leaves flitter into the mush,
we saw joggers with babies in buggies,
we saw women in burkas
like black letter boxes.

This mixture of people thrills me.

I love that sycamore somersault,
acorn attack. There may be spring.

Come with me again across the park;
it is ours, a garden of earthly delight.

And we're not expelled. Yet.

The Wrong Woman

You take too much. I'd rather you paid your way
even if the sex is good. But even then you go cold

after you've come. Why shouldn't I get lucky?

You'd be surprised by my disconsolacy,
put it down to my age or my demands.

You will not soon find pleasure from my hands.

For David Albert, my Dad

You were a blue-eyed, handsome man,
Dapper in your uniform.
No wonder Lily fell for you:
A cut above the usual crew.

If I could, I'd buy you caravans
Across the world, clear blue skies.
Crystal streams, dark green forests,
Bluebells as beautiful as your eyes.

But I've no money, only a willing heart
And my magic daughter. That's a start.

Uncle Billy

Polished his shoes underneath. Wore braces,
went so far as to say:
"Yes, I will have another tart, please, Edie".
Wore a homburg. We boys made faces:

this was unfair in the light of the Bournville bar
with a sellotaped red, ten shilling note,
which arrived each Boxing Day, as did Billy.
In younger days, he'd travelled far

on a motorbike. Before that to the Somme,
Where he did as he was told, kept a straight bat.
He loved my grandma Edie: she married Charlie instead.
Billy lived in Acton Town. In a flat.

A Loaf past its sell-by date
For Amanda Porter

Squidgy white, with a thin crust. Sunblest,
like you, my dear friend or like I'd like you to be.
Not like a paraplegic George Best,
not like a gargoyle with whelky skin.

Not, I suppose, like me.

What can a man expect of a day …
                    which begins with getting up in the morning?

These yellowing leaves do not console. The heron wings
into the milky blue, spears breakfast from the Calder.
and slow as snails the tots trail their mums to school.

I was wearing my Doctor Who scarf and a seven year old
swang on it. "Are you Bob Dylan?" "No, I'm Peter,
what's your name?" "Tina." Some leaves are gold.

Towards the Rainbow in Bradford

A tiny woman with a plastic bag
skitters across Manningham Lane. Cars squeal,
snarl, splash. In a phone box that bright eyed youth
makes contact. Meanwhile there's a cirrus scrawl,
a cumulonimbus ceiling, the fat, wet feel of rain.

It's a steep hill, but as sycamores spiral
squashed plastic bottles spin, you might think
someone spoke through the fall. Just keep going,
like the man with the sequinned beret,
who scatters seed for the pigeons, like the dog,
half Alsatian, half Dachshund, pissing in the wind.

Do not forget that over the tops
Charlotte, Emily, Anne and Branwell
played toy soldiers and checked out early.

Their gravestones carved in our own hearts.

Towards the Sun in Bradford

You'd squint when a young girl gives you the eye,
her jean skirt barely below her groin.
Thirty pounds will buy you fifteen minutes -
but come now, she's someone's daughter, someone's
mother. And you don't really know her name.
A syringe drinks the brown puddle in the car park.

You'd quicken your pace when the pit bull
yanks its pit bull down Manningham Lane,
Union Jack tattooed on both buttocks.

You'd smile at Ali, who's moved here from Leeds;
and the sun doesn't shine, it weeps, it bleeds.

The Terrible Twins
For Rene and Dennis Greig

Mad as spoons, that's what my scruffy friend Brendan says
and so you are. You'd keep a menagerie of llamas,
a scoop of melted ice-cream, a country
of refugees in your back yard. You construct plays
out of conflict, take children from war zones
into safe havens, play pens, your own home.

I think you try to do too much,
which nearly kills you. But why live
unless you give, why give unless you forgive,
why strive without a blithe blink at the touch
of chance? I love the way you love your kids:

I think of you on the beach at Bangor,
dancing like starfish, dropping a danger.

Black Sheep in the White Swan

He might have been a promenade concert:
Loved to walk the moors, is grieved by many.
Elizabeth Anne and Henry Wood will flirt
In heaven, like cherubs, like bright pennies.

The White Swan. A haven for the half lost,
Shiny brass, not the smallest speck of dust.
Look at the prices! If you're tempest-tossed,
Launch into the lamb chops. Cheap at twice the cost.

Henry was dapper, precise, five foot eight,
Rose to a full two yards in his voice,
Like a white swan, sings still for his mate.
Has no choice.

Some people think he's still here:
That must be the crazy Black Sheep beer.

The White Swan. It won't welcome just anyone,
Fine manners are a must. And dignity,
And trust. A Yorkshire pud of gentle fun,
English as mustard, a buttered currant bun.

A Pink Toutou
For my daughter

Snap! Suddenly the world was safe and simple:
Tin soldiers slept easy in their boxes,
The night whispered with happy endings,
Answered prayers. No lonely soul but breathed peace,
Peace like a chill wind across shallow waters.

If you move, move no more than an eyebrow,
If you speak, speak on tiptoe, speak low,
Do not break the spell. Today's the birthday
of tomorrow. Love will tell you what to say.